The Lost S

by Anne Giulieri
illustrated by Martin Bailey

"Look, Dad!" said Kate.
"My sock is not here."

3

"Look!" said Dad.

"Here is a pink sock.

Here is a green sock, too."

"I can look
for the lost socks,"
said Dad.

Dad looked and looked.

"Here is the green sock,"
said Dad.
"Here is the pink sock, too!"

"Look!" shouted Dad.
"Here is **my** sock."

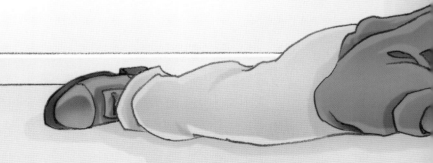

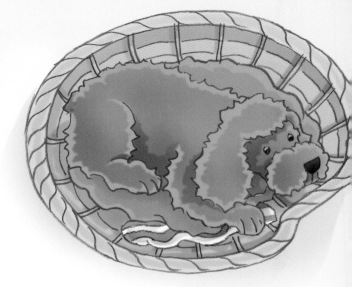

Kate looked too.

"Dad," said Kate.

"This is not my sock."

13

"Look, Dad!" shouted Kate.
"Here is Max
and here is **my** lost sock!"

"Look at my socks!"
said Kate.